Ricky Roars

Ricky Roars

Signs Of Love From Beyond

Elison McAllaster

BALBOA.
PRESS

A DIVISION OF HAY HOUSE

Balboa Press books may be ordered through booksellers or by contacting:

Balboa Press
A Division of Hay House
1663 Liberty Drive
Bloomington, IN 47403
www.balboapress.com
1-(877) 407-4847

Because of the dynamic nature of the Internet, any web addresses or
links contained in this book may have changed since publication and
may no longer be valid. The views expressed in this work are solely those
of the author and do not necessarily reflect the views of the publisher,
and the publisher hereby disclaims any responsibility for them.

The author of this book does not dispense medical advice or prescribe the use
of any technique as a form of treatment for physical, emotional, or medical
problems without the advice of a physician, either directly or indirectly. The
intent of the author is only to offer information of a general nature to help
you in your quest for emotional and spiritual well-being. In the event you use
any of the information in this book for yourself, which is your constitutional
right, the author and the publisher assume no responsibility for your actions.

Any people depicted in stock imagery provided by Thinkstock are
models, and such images are being used for illustrative purposes only.

Certain stock imagery © Thinkstock.

Cover design, "Galaxy", courtesy of Ann Marie McAllaster, Spring, 2011.

ISBN: 978-1-4525-3802-0 (e)
ISBN: 978-1-4525-3801-3 (sc)

Printed in the United States of America

Balboa Press rev. date: 9/23/2011

This book is dedicated to our shooting star, Ricky McAllaster. He taught us how to live every second of every day, how to laugh as if it's our last breath, how to love with all our hearts, and most importantly, how to share love after leaving this Earth.

CONTENTS

Contents

"God doesn't give you the people you want; he gives you the people you *need* . . .

To help you, to hurt you, to love you, to leave you, and to make you into the person you were meant to be." Lee Suarez

CHAPTER ONE

Pivotal Moments

"Aha" moments. Pivotal moments. Quantum leaps. Life-changing events.

Many of us have had them. Moments that rip away, even if just for a second, the thick curtain of illusion that we're in charge, that our minds and our drive and our egos can control our lives—what happens to us and when. If we're lucky, this parting of the curtain allows us a glimpse into the blinding light, action, and script of the greater plan for our lives. Your life will never be the same; change is inevitable.

Our pivotal moment came at 2:12 a.m. on January 1, 2010. At any second, another person's choices can totally change your life. Our metamorphosis started on New Year's Eve—every parent's nightmare.

My husband, Dick, and I were home with our nineteen-year-old daughter, fifteen-year-old son, and several of their friends, thinking that our master plan of everyone being on lockdown for the night would keep everyone safe. The kids were setting off fireworks on the dock, and we were inside peacefully watching the after midnight celebrations on TV. After the firework's noise stopped, my husband went outside to check on everyone. I heard him out in the front yard loudly talking with the kids, then he made some cell phone calls. A second later, I heard a loud metallic boom and chuckled to myself, thinking that in the dark Dick had walked into the grill. I heard him frantically call my name, and as I looked out the window, I saw his car fly out the driveway. Within two minutes, my husband, a six-foot tall, successful, respected stockbroker, sports addict, coach, and ex-hockey player, was on the phone with me, sobbing so hard I couldn't understand him.

My life as I knew it was forever changed when he finally managed to gasp out the two words I will forever hear echoing in my head and heart.

"Ricky's dead."

CHAPTER TWO
A Son to be Proud of

Life has a way of mocking our plans sometimes. Our fifteen-year-old youngest son, Ricky, was a son to be proud of. We were chosen to be his adoptive parents after his birth mother interviewed over thirty couples. We flew to Salt Lake City, Utah, from Georgia to pick up Ricky. With his bright green eyes, long, lanky body, ever present grin, pop-out ears, and mischievous, inquisitive personality, Ricky was a constant challenge to keep up with. His energy and zest for life were unequaled. During his toddler years, nothing was safe around him. His preschool teacher worried about a heart attack as he led the class in shelf-jumping stunts. As I chased him from room to room while he stuck his fingers in every wall outlet, drew with permanent markers down the hallway walls, teased the family dog, climbed and jumped off every shelf and piece of furniture, and totally, thoroughly exhausted me, I wondered how I could possibly satisfy his insatiable curiosity and energy. I would joke with friends that Ricky would grow up thinking his name was "No!" since that was all I ever seemed to say to him. But, just like Dennis the Menace, he was so full of life, love, and laughter that he stole everyone's heart.

Ricky was a challenge and a joy, a pain and a pleasure, an aggravation and an inspiration. To me, he was the epitome of the duality of life. He grew into a nerve-wracking, rule-breaking, adrenaline-seeking teen who simply wanted to love, laugh, and spend time with his friends. He tormented his older sister, Ann Marie, endlessly by constantly trying to hang out with her friends, and he never met a person he didn't like. He insisted on living life on the edge and was an unstoppable free spirit. Nothing was too high, too scary, or too difficult for him to master, and any challenge was meant to be conquered. On his fifth grade yearbook page, I quoted the actor he reminded me of: James Dean. "Dream as if you'll live forever. Live as if you'll die today." That was our life with Ricky.

By the time he was six, we were able to semi-retire, and we moved to a Colorado ski resort. Ricky's incredible athletic ability was seen early in life as a roller hockey goalie, so he found his home in the extreme sports offered in Colorado. By age twelve, he had competed and won as a Colorado state runner-up champion ice hockey goalie, a cross country and downhill mountain biker (he qualified for the Nationals as a nine year old), a snowboard team racer (was the third-ranked boarder in his age bracket in the state of Colorado), and played left attack man in lacrosse (three-time middle school All Star player).

He had absolutely no fear, and was a fierce warrior in all sports. His aggressive nature, demand for his own and others personal best, natural athleticism, and restless energy made him a fierce competitor. The shelves in his room were overflowing with trophies, ribbons, plaques, and autographed posters. Our lives consisted of endless driving to tournaments, races, or practices for whatever sport he was mastering. Not to mention visits to emergency rooms with broken bones!

We had to move back to Georgia when Ricky was twelve, and he was very bored with Southern sports. He had grown up loving extreme speed, flying forty feet in the air over snow packed jumps, the adrenaline rush of four hockey players crashing in to score on him, and blasting down a double black diamond ski run in the summer on his mountain bike, passing rocks and trees in an exhilarating blur. In Georgia, he was too skinny to be a force on the football field, even though he picked up the game fast. He tried golf and shot a hole in one on the last hole of his last middle school tournament after only playing for eight months. He won the Coach's Choice award his first season on the middle school golf team. He played basketball and started showing promise in that sport also. He loved boating, kneeboarding, tubing, and diving head first off of our dock into the water, but his greatest pride was the fishing boat we bought him at age fourteen. He loved the speed and thrill of pushing his boat to its limits as he flew over the water.

Ricky missed the adrenaline rush and contact of fast sports, so he and his father dedicated themselves to helping expand middle school lacrosse in our area. Within a year, Ricky had encouraged so many of his friends to play the sport that his middle school team went from losing every game to winning every tournament.

He transferred to a local boy's military school in his freshman year of high school, and within two months, his infectious smile and personality had enough boys signed up to field the first high school varsity lacrosse team in town. Ricky became known in the area as an outstanding lacrosse player—he was the first high school freshman ever picked to play on the local elite high school travel team and started receiving scholarship letters from colleges to play for them before he finished his first semester of high school.

The game of lacrosse was invented by the American Indians as a training drill for their warriors to stay in shape and practice their fighting skills, so it was a natural choice for our warrior son. His style of play, his flamboyant personality, and his looks earned him the nickname "Hollywood" from coaches and parents who watched him.

Ricky seemed to live a charmed life when it came to friends and girls. He never met a person that he didn't immediately approach like they were best friends, and he seemed to live solely to meet as many people as he could. His social life was a frenetic buzz, and he exhausted his friends with nonstop entertainment. There was no time to rest, lounge in front of the TV, or just be quiet. Life was meant to be jammed with action, activity, other people, and girls, girls, girls, every minute of every day. He was always the life of the party, and his friends counted on him to think up ways to fill their days with fun, people, and laughter. Any time he would complain to me about being bored, I would suggest just sitting down to read a book or listen to music. His "Are you crazy?" look was well known to me. Every night his homework study sessions would consist of sitting at his desk while posting on his Facebook page, one earplug in while listening to his iPod, talking on his cell phone on speaker, and briefly looking at the open book in front of him. I would get dizzy just thinking about keeping up with all that activity.

In hindsight, Ricky's high energy level, determination, and his incredible capacity for love explain the many events that have happened to us over the past year. He always found a way to do whatever he wanted to do, no matter the cost.

Five days before the first high school lacrosse team practice, Ricky stole his sister's car and left our home to meet some girls. Returning home at an excessive rate of speed, he failed to make a sharp corner. The car skidded sideways into a double thick concrete block wall. True to his warrior nature and his reckless, Mach One pace of living, he was not wearing a seat belt.

He was two driveways away from our home.

CHAPTER THREE

Our Shooting Star

The agony of losing a child, especially one so loved by all and so full of life and potential, is beyond unbearable. Beyond reality. Beyond any experience of pain I have ever known. Beyond description.

As Ann Marie and I ran to the accident site, I prayed that Dick had been wrong. As soon as I saw the car on its side, lying in the midst of the swirling fog and violently exploded concrete wall, I heard a strange animal keening sound as my guts were being ripped in half. My stomach heaved relentlessly, my head spun, and I had to hang onto my husband as I collapsed. I later realized it was me making that animalistic, pain-filled noise. Ann Marie staggered off to the side as her body was racked with nausea. Shock and a separation from reality is the mind's natural defense, and I couldn't focus on what had really happened. I couldn't cry. It just wasn't real; it couldn't be true. Did this really happen to us, to our Ricky? As I stared at the huge hole in the wall, I felt the vast emptiness of the even larger hole that had been ripped open in my heart, body, and soul. I felt so empty, so hollow, so unable to face the coming pain in our lives.

As I slowly realized that our Ricky was truly gone from us, I looked up at the bright, star-filled sky and declared what I knew to be true: "He was our shooting star." Our beloved Ricky burned hot, fast, and bright through our lives, and then was gone.

To this day, I don't know what motivated me to do this, but I turned to Dick and looked directly into his eyes. Something told me to reach up and hold his face between my hands. With all my strength, I told him that we had to believe that this happened for more good than negative—it had to be. That is how the Universe works. This action turned out to be our saving grace.

Dick needed to cry; he needed to express himself to me; he needed to let it all out, or we were not going to be able to make it through this together. He nodded as the tears rolled down his cheeks, unable to say anything. We stood there like that, holding on to each other.

As the paramedics and policemen arrived and tried to shield us from the macabre sight, we became aware of one policeman focusing on us, soothing us, and making waving motions with his arms as he walked around us, herding us, pushing us into a circle and encouraging us to hold onto each other. I felt comfortable having someone tell us what to do, how to handle this tragedy, how to proceed beyond that horrible moment. We had no idea what to do next. As he continued slowly speaking, walking around us, and waving his arms in a circular motion, I felt that he was making inward waving motions like a mother bird's wings, pulling her babies into the protection of her body. We were being pushed together into a familial circle of love and security. A few days later I realized that his motions were like a slowly flapping, extended angel's wings, folding us together into safety and comfort, as in Psalm 91: 4: "He shall cover thee with his feathers, and under his wings shall thou trust." Little did I know that this was just the first of many healing, miraculous events sent to us that would soothe our pain.

CHAPTER FOUR

Stand with Faith

Our story is not only about how to switch your reactions to life's tragic events, but also about how we were led to open our eyes and hearts to the love and support around us. Our conscious choice to look for the good, to strive every day through our tears and grief to trust that God would take care of us, is what saved us. Our faith gave us the strength to trust that things happen for the greater good of all and to make it through our darkest days by looking forward to days of laughter and love again.

In this life, we cannot change what others choose to do to us, but we can choose how we react. That is our free will in action. My favorite bumper sticker says, "How you treat me is your karma. How I react is mine."

The band Rascal Flats' song *Stand* inspired us to stand strong, to fight against whatever feelings were dragging us down. Dick and I knew that we still had our lives to live, just as Ricky had his life to live and his choices to make. In Ricky's memory, we chose to be warriors, to stand strong, to defeat and throw off the burden of grief, and to honor our son's strength, passion, and zest for life in order to keep him close to us. What you have been doesn't matter; it's what you choose to become from your life experiences that's important.

The renowned psychic Char advises us how to defeat any negativity and despair. In her book *Questions from Earth, Answers from Heaven*, she tells us to visualize wrapping ourselves in God's pure white light to protect us and to push away any darkness and negative forces by declaring, "In the name of God, be gone." This is a powerful tool that I have used many times to stay focused on what is good and positive around me.

Einstein's relativity theory and more recent quantum physics findings support my beliefs about what happens after we leave this life. The basic scientific law of conservation of energy states: "Energy cannot be created nor destroyed. It can only be transformed from one state to another." The only thing that can happen to energy is that it can change form: for instance, chemical energy can become kinetic energy. In Wikipedia's explanation of the law of conservation of energy we read that matter, such as that constituting atoms, can be converted to non-matter forms of energy, such as light. Our true selves, our souls, are pure energy, and we do not cease to exist when we die. Only our physical bodies die.

We all are spiritual beings living in a physical body. Rest assured that your loved ones aren't gone; they're simply in another form of energy.

I believe in a greater Good, or God, or Allah, or Buddha, or whatever name you choose to call the power of good that is within us, around us, everywhere and in everything. I believe that people are inherently good. I believe there is a purpose to our lives here. We are born to be tested, to learn and grow, to find the good within ourselves and in other people, and to help others find the good within themselves. This is the simple, noble purpose to our lives.

Why do we experience pain? Pain brings knowledge and growth because it makes us question things. We wondered, Why Ricky? Why our family? Why would God take such an incredible, giving child so soon? Why do we have to live without the satisfaction that we did our job as parents and protected this child from harm? Why do we have to live with this hole in our hearts? What did we do to deserve this?

The questions, anger, and frustration could drive you mad if you don't have faith. Faith that God is with us, always helping us learn and grow. He is orchestrating our lives for our personal growth toward good and the good of others. Faith brings knowledge and release from pain, for it helps us trust and look for the good that comes in time. We have to be very patient, trust that positive will outweigh negative, and keep our eyes open for signs of love and comfort all around us.

Dick and I worked every day to push aside our heavy load of sorrow and guilt, and to be happy in the knowledge that our incredible son was in a better place, happy and finally free to soar as high and as fast as he desired. We tried to not question why this had happened, and to focus on the good that we were expecting to be shown us. A good friend told us of Matt Dickerson's saying: "Don't put a question mark where God has put a period." We are sharing our positive experiences so that others may find hope and peace in the signs we were shown.

Our signs of comfort were so obvious that we were jolted into realizing that we were being taken care of. We realized we had no sorrow for Ricky—he was surrounded by love. We had to trust that the tragic event on our New Year's Eve would benefit far more people than just our little family. We were shown that we are all on this Earth together, that all those we meet and interact with are connected, and that there are no accidents. We are not alone. Everything happens for a reason.

After we walked home from the accident site on the morning of Jan 1, 2010 (later seen as 01-01-10 as we studied numerology), we stayed up the rest of the night talking to the police, welcoming friends and family into our house of pain and shock, and trying to find room for the flood of food and people pouring through our doors. Family from Washington, North Carolina, Florida, and all over Georgia arrived to try to comfort us and help us cope. We were totally numb, alternating between crying and zombie-like shock, and trying to let everyone know how much we appreciated their love and concern.

Our oldest son, George, never left my side, hovering over me, holding me up if I even started to quiver or shake and trying to get me to eat. By midday on New Year's Day, he started telling me that we needed to go back to the accident site to see what Ricky's friends had created. I never wanted to see that wall again, but George kept insisting that it would do me good to go look. We had to go and see what his friends had done.

Finally Dick and I agreed to get out of the house, thinking that some fresh air would help clear our heads. Ann Marie was in her room with about twelve girlfriends who were sleeping over and helping her, so we got her up, threw on some coats, and walked over to the hole in the wall. I will never forget what we saw.

At least two hundred of Ricky's friends had gathered in the freezing cold. They each brought with them flowers, candles, pictures, and mementos of their good times with Ricky—a movie he liked, ice skates, lacrosse helmets, jerseys, the cologne he wore, a piece of a SeaDoo, or whatever they felt represented their personal memories and time with Ricky. Many of them were writing poems, messages of love, or poignant sayings on the many large chunks of concrete scattered over the site. The violence of the impact could almost be physically felt as we stared at the various pieces of car parts flung everywhere around the site, the pieces of concrete that had been blasted to a powder, and the bent rebar showing the path of the car's flight. The harsh physical evidence was in sharp contrast to the quiet, somber group of so many devastated teenagers huddled closely together, hugging each other and crying. About twenty of Ricky's best friends from his military school had gathered in a semicircle behind the shrine they had built, arms around each other as they cried. When we walked up, they struggled through singing the school fight song for us, for their fallen comrade. We stood there speechless, overwhelmed by their love and pain, and the emotions surrounding us all.

wreck site

After we thanked all of the teens and started to walk off, a disheveled-looking man stepped forward out of the crowd and addressed the boys. We didn't know him, but I listened to him as we walked away. He asked the boys and girls to tell him something about Ricky, something funny, so he could get to know him better. I was intrigued and asked my family to turn around with me so we could listen. Ricky's friends were puzzled but slowly began to tell stories that started to bring smiles to our faces as we honored the good, crazy, goofy fifteen-year-old whom we had loved. I even stepped forward and told a funny story. After we finished talking, this gentle man, a complete stranger to us all, thanked everyone for sharing their memories and advised us to hold on to that love, that warm smile that came with the memories, and remember the good times. His final words shocked me, as I had not been able to stop asking myself and God, *Why Ricky?* He said, "We may not understand why, but sometimes someone's greatest strength is their greatest weakness."

His words were exactly what I needed to hear. I knew that the only thing that would draw Ricky from the safety of our home that night was his lifelong compulsion to share good times with as many people as possible and to be with as many girls as possible. His avid need for speed was what killed him.

As this stranger turned to us and introduced himself as Don Dilley, I asked him where he came from. His answer rocked us.

The night before, as we walked back to our home from the accident site, I told Dick," Oh my God, Dick, we don't have a minister to bury Ricky!" Our favorite local minister had died while we were living in Colorado, and we hadn't really connected with any others in town. We became lazy and stopped going to church. I justified this by considering myself a good person who didn't need to attend church to worship God, yet there we were living in the southern Bible Belt without a family minister! Dick understood my concern that night, but we just didn't have the energy or time to do anything about it.

As I talked to Don and asked him more about himself, he explained that he was a retired Presbyterian minister who had recently decided to fulfill his lifelong dream of travelling on his sailboat to the Bahamas. Don had been peacefully cruising off the Georgia coast on Christmas Eve when his GPS mysteriously failed. His boat ran aground on some jetties and started to sink. Don had frantically called every marine tow service he could locate, and the one service who would come out on that special holiday would only tow him—of course—to the marina right next door to Ricky's accident site. His boat had extensive damage, and Don had spent five days cleaning up mud and debris from the bottom of it. He wondered why he had ended up there, but trusted that his fate would be revealed.

Remember, there are no accidents. Both Dick and I grew up in the Presbyterian faith. As I listened to Don's story, I began to realize that God had sent us our minister! Not only did He send us a minister, but He literally had him right there on site waiting for us.

In my amazement over this "coincidence", I invited Don to come home with us for some food and warmth.

We talked for hours, introduced him to our family and friends, and he agreed to help us with all the preparations for the memorial service. We were so thankful to have him there right when we needed him that we referred to him as "our second angel" sent to help us within twenty-four hours.

We now know that Don was so touched by being able to help us and by the joy he received in ministering again that he decided to move from retirement to active status in the Presbyterian church. He is now an interim minister in our community, has repaired his sailboat, and is free once again to take off for the Bahamas. But Don has decided he likes Georgia and plans to stay for a few years to see where God takes him. We usually never know the impact our decisions have on other's lives, but in our case, we have been allowed to witness the good.

On New Year's Eve, before we left the accident site, our policeman friend asked if he could visit us the next day. We wanted to repay his kindness and encouraged him to visit. He showed up the next day and presented to my husband a heavy bronze coin. It was engraved with the Bomb Squad logo on one side, and the other side quoted part of Isaiah 6:8, "Here am I; send me." He told my husband to keep it in his pocket at all times, for it would protect him. We later learned that this coin was not freely given to Bomb Squad members; they had to earn it. This gift so impressed my husband that he carried it everywhere with him, constantly turning it over in his hands, wondering what the purpose of this gift would be.

About two months after Ricky's death, we decided to become actively involved in teen driving safety programs. At three in the morning, my husband had an idea. We created bronze key chains for every teenager in town to carry. These key chains have an image of Ricky's smiling face in the middle, with bold red letters printed on a diagonal that read, "THINK." We felt very strongly that the weight of this key chain might help a teenager think twice before driving home after partying too much.

THINK keychain

Our nephews also ordered glow in the dark memory wristbands for Ricky's friends to wear that read, "Rest in Peace Ricky, 01/01/10." We have given out hundreds of these wristbands, and we tell the teenagers to wear these bands on their right wrist so they will glow brightly at night as the car keys are turned in the ignition. We realize that we cannot stop underage drinking and driving, but we hope that at least one teen will stop and think of the consequences of a bad choice. Our THINK campaign is spreading to other towns, and we continue to work with teen driving safety programs. The compassion of that one policeman generated the spark of an idea that helped create for hundreds of teens a lifesaving reminder of a friend gone too soon.

Chapter Five

God's Wonders

As comforting as it was to meet these two very special men, we had no idea how incredible our journey toward healing would become. Our pain and sorrow were replaced by wonder and hope about thirty-six hours after Ricky's passing. Our life became an example of Daniel 4:2 which states "I thought it good to show the sights and wonders that the high God hath wrought toward me."

On January 2, 2010, we were at home with family members after finally sleeping some, crying a lot, and generally wondering how we were going to survive this ordeal. Ricky had four of his close friends at our house on New Year's Eve. They ran to the crash site with us that night and stood vigil in the cold by the demolished car for over four hours until the body was retrieved. On that January 2, these boys were down the street from our house, sitting around on a dock, talking and crying. Suddenly, out of nowhere, a wild pelican flew down onto the dock next to them. It stood there looking at them, and then started walking around between them. It didn't fly away when they stood to take pictures or walked up to it; it didn't fly away when they stooped to pet it, and it didn't fly away when Zack hugged it and picked it up in his arms. They all took pictures with their cell phones to record this incredible visit.

This wild creature, a deadly hunter of fish, stayed on the dock with them for over thirty minutes, walking around between them, hanging out, and playing with them. The boys were absolutely convinced that it was Ricky coming back to tease them, just like he always used to.

Initial pelican visitation

As soon as the pelican flew away, the boys rushed down to our house to tell us what had just happened.

They showed us their pictures of the pelican standing next to them, and even one of Zack holding the pelican in his arms and hugging it. I had never heard of such a thing—wild pelicans are very aloof and solitary birds. The boys were convinced that it was Ricky in the bird's body, and he was visiting with them. I had goose bumps all over me as I looked at their pictures, but as much as I wanted to believe that it was my larger than life son inhabiting the bird's body, I didn't want to tell them that could happen. We hugged and laughed a lot, and after they left, we talked and wondered about that amazing occurrence.

We saw a lot of pelicans around our dock over the next four days, but we live on a coastal river so we didn't think that much of it. We were busy struggling through our tears to plan the memorial service, pick out the urn for his ashes, and planning a funeral service. On Thursday, January 7, my husband and I, Ann Marie and her boyfriend, and Don drove through the cemetery entrance for the funeral. Ann Marie and I were both looking out the side window of the car and noticed about twelve or fifteen pelicans standing in a line, almost in formation, along the side of a nearby drainage ditch. We both commented on it, since it was unusual to see pelicans in town that far from water, plus they were standing in such a formal lineup. It was later that we realized the symbolism of their military salute.

We endured the burial, and as we were driving out the cemetery gates, we looked to see if the pelicans were still there. As soon as we commented on their absence, Ann Marie's boyfriend said, "Oh, no, there was a pelican at the graveside." As we whipped our heads around to stare at him in wonder, he told us there had been a lone pelican walking among the headstones during the service. It had stopped several times behind our funeral tent, almost as if it were listening. None of us knew what to say, but we all knew this was too much to be just a coincidence.

We drove home and started preparing lunch for our large family. Before George joined us to hear about the pelicans at the cemetery, he went to his house to pick up more food for our lunch. He called me from his house and said, "Mom, what is it about pelicans?" I couldn't speak for a minute, but then I said, "Ummm, I don't know—why?" He told me there were two pelicans standing in his driveway as he drove up to his home, and they weren't flying away. As we were talking on the phone, George walked up to the pelicans and they didn't leave; they just walked around him. He took pictures of the pelicans standing in his driveway that day.

more pelicans

I stood there in awe as my son hung up. I majored in English in college, and something in my sleep-deprived brain made me wonder about the religious symbolism of pelicans. My sister-in-law searched on the Internet and came back into the room wide-eyed and excited. Pelicans have been honored for centuries, as far back as Egyptian times, as symbols of parental and maternal solicitude. It was believed that in times of famine, the adult pelican would shred its breast with its long, curved bill and feed its young its own flesh and blood. This has since been proven not true, but these birds are still honored as a symbol of piety, self-sacrifice, and virtue. They were adopted by the Christian church as symbols of the live-giving sacrifice of Christ, or of the Eucharist. Many stained glass windows and altar frontals in Christian churches have pelicans in them.

As we listened to this explanation of all our visitations by pelicans, it slowly began to dawn on us that our life after Ricky's passing was not going to be the normal experience. Just as life with Ricky had not been normal, so life after Ricky wasn't going to be normal! Slowly, we began to feel that we were being taken care of. I cannot say whether it was God, our guardian angels, or Ricky himself sending us our miraculous pelican visits, but knowing that we were being sent obvious, repeated signs of comfort and everlasting love helped push aside our pain and feelings of loss, and flooded us with wonder and amazement. We began to look forward to the days ahead, feeling curious and alive again, and filled with gratitude for our signs of love.

As months passed, we had many more visitations by pelicans, and they always showed when we needed comforting. Ann Marie has always felt a strong connection to the beautiful, graceful Atlantic bottlenose dolphins that are so numerous on our coastline. Around January 14, Ann Marie bravely decided that she would go back to college to be with her friends. We told her that we would go with her and make sure that she was comfortable, so I went upstairs in our bedroom to pack. We have a large row of windows that face the river, and as I looked out, I was awestruck once again. There, almost as if they were dancing together, were six pelicans swooping up and down over the water while three bottlenose dolphins surfaced and played underneath them. I called my family upstairs to witness the celebration orchestrated through Ricky's love, a joyous victory dance of our daughter's decision to resume her life.

About a month later, Dick and I travelled to our magical healing place, the beautiful island of St. Simon's, Georgia. We wanted some beach time together on Valentine's Day. As we stopped to eat lunch at the oceanside buffet at the King and Prince hotel, we were entertained by a pelican hunting over the water at the beach, right in front of our window. That lone pelican seemed to be showing off his acrobatic and hunting skills just for us—a lot like our cocky son. He caught one fish, swallowed it, then continued cruising, banking sharply into turns, and swooping down close to the water. It was a spectacular display of his flying and fishing skills, and reminded us of how free and happy our son is now.

Another day I was driving down a busy four lane highway in town, talking on my cell phone as I tried to console a friend of Ricky's who had just lost another friend. I sensed something and looked to the left out my car window. There, in the middle of town, on a busy four lane street, a pelican was flying down the median staying parallel with the driver side of my car!

In March, my niece and I were enjoying the warmer spring weather by walking around a lake in town. My niece had lost her mother about five years earlier, and we were consoling each other and discussing how to carry on with life after experiencing such pain. We both noticed a pelican floating in the lake, surrounded by ducks and Canadian geese. There are usually many ducks and geese in that lake, but never a pelican that far in town. We both smiled, threw our arms around each other, and continued our walk with love in our hearts.

My most recent visit happened on December 22, 2010. We had finally healed enough to have an oyster roast at our house with over seventy-five friends. Ricky always loved it when we entertained, especially when we had oysters followed by roasted S'mores over the fire pit. I went down onto our dock the next morning to throw out some leftover food to the crabs. It was a beautiful, crisp day, so I decided to walk up onto our sun deck to enjoy the quiet and the invigorating panoramic view of our green marshes and sun-sparkled waters. As I leaned over the railing, I sensed something. I looked up, and right over my head were twenty two pelicans flying in a V formation. They were so quiet I sensed them rather than heard them. I was filled with joy and appreciation for the beauty and serenity of God's creations, and the comforting presence of the pelicans. I have never seen that many pelicans together, and not since.

These visitations from pelicans initiated our healing process. They helped console us, soothed our pain, and filled our broken hearts with the warm knowledge that divine love will find you when you need it the most. You only need to ask, and trust.

Chapter Six

Love from Beyond this World

Many books have been published recently giving amazing accounts of people sensing their passed loved ones near them, smelling them, feeling a soft touch, being visited in dreams, and various inexplicable electronic signals. These accounts attest to the increasing awareness of a new age when the western world will accept that there is more to life than what we're traditionally taught. We should try to use our intuition and senses to stay in touch and never fear our loved ones contacts. They try to let us know they are still with us, try to help, and send their never ending love. Both Dick and I have had many experiences of messages from beyond, and we know without a doubt that these contacts are real from the very warm, personal nature of the messages we received.

Dick had a very vivid dream visitation on February 2, 2010. Dick never remembers his dreams, but this one was etched crystal clear in his mind when he woke. He dreamed that he walked into a convenience store and saw Ricky standing there. This is humorous to us since Ricky always begged to stop at every convenience store he saw so he could buy a sweet snack. Dick asked him, "Ricky, where have you been?" Ricky nonchalantly said, "Don't worry Dad; I'm just off at camp." He told Dick that he needed a snow day, then was gone.

This visitation was filled with so much meaning for us. Ricky's love of sweet snacks from convenience stores was notorious. His reference to "being off at camp" had great healing symbolism, for Ricky loved the adventure of leaving home to go off to sports camps. He actually loved any chance for a new adventure! We knew this message meant he was having fun away at a camp-like experience, and that we would be together again soon. His snow day reference was important because we had been trying to pick a time for a family trip to Colorado to spread some of Ricky's ashes on a snowboard jump. Ricky was telling Dick that he wanted us to do that for him and for us.

One example of a dream visitation happened to me twenty-three days after Ricky left us. On Ricky's fifteenth birthday, when I took him for his learners permit test, he was so thrilled that he could be an organ donor that he talked about it all the way home. The night Ricky passed, we were not able to donate his organs since his body had been trapped in the car for so long, but we were able to donate his eyes and tissues. As we spoke with a Georgia Eye Bank representative and confirmed that we wanted to make that donation, I asked if we could be notified of a successful transplant. Ricky had the most beautiful, glowing green eyes! As his mother, I desperately wanted to see those eyes shining at me one more time. We were told to send the manager our request in writing, and she would try to contact us after a successful transplant. Due to our complicated privacy laws, no names or other information could be given. I prayed and cried many times for a chance to see his beautiful, loving eyes again.

For many months after Ricky passed, I woke up every night at precisely 2:08 AM, which is the exact time that Ricky hit the wall. At 2:08 am on January 24, 2010, I was roused by a repeated sound like a cell phone making a bell ringing sound, then making the sound of a vibrating phone. I checked the time and wasn't surprised to be aroused at that morbid time, but I lay there wondering about the bell ringing sound I had heard. Neither my cell phone nor my husband's phone was set to that ringtone, and they were both in the bathroom on the chargers. I lay there for a few minutes puzzling over what I had heard, but since I didn't hear it anymore, I closed my eyes to try to go back to sleep.

Immediately, I saw very clearly an image of a black horse approaching with a rider. It was just like seeing animals and people in your dreams, but I knew I wasn't dreaming since I had just closed my eyes. I have loved horses since birth, and they have always been a source of comfort and therapy for me. I was intrigued, for at that time I owned a black Friesian, and this horse resembled a Friesian with its high head and proud stature. As I noticed that, the horse took a step closer, and I saw that the rider was a corpse. It was neither ghoulish nor scary, but simply a dead body sitting on a black horse. As a riding instructor, I noticed and wondered about the rider's hand position, for the hands were together, high and stiff out in front of the body with palms upturned. As I looked even closer, I saw an olive branch draped across the corpse's hands. Then, just as quickly as the image appeared, it vanished. I instantly sat up in bed, wondering what I had just seen and why I had seen it?

Obviously the olive branch was a symbol of peace, so I wondered if I had just been given a peace offering from beyond. I stayed awake for a long time thinking about what had happened and then wrote down what I had seen and felt.

Ricky's eyes

The very next day we received a telephone call from the manager of the Georgia Eye Bank telling us that they had successfully transplanted one of Ricky's eyes, and the other eye was being used for research. My prayers had been answered. I finally found peace knowing that not only would I recognize Ricky's bright green eye one day when we meet again, but also that somewhere in Georgia one of Ricky's eyes had renewed the gift of sight for another soul.

In the first days after Ricky's death, I was tormented with doubt that our son had not been able to pass over due to the immense sorrow and pain his friends were suffering. I didn't know where to turn to get answers, so a friend suggested we contact a psychic medium. We felt anything was worth a try, so we made an appointment with Catherine Crabtree, a psychic medium in Charlotte, North Carolina. On January 12, 2010, just twelve short days after losing Ricky, Dick and I, along with our daughter, contacted him. There is absolutely no doubt in any of our minds that it was Ricky coming through. I decided to take notes since I knew there would be a lot of tears, and I'm thankful I did, for his messages, humor, and words of encouragement console us to this day.

The first image the psychic picked up was a container of marbles or small balls. We couldn't understand what she was talking about, but as she kept describing what she was seeing, she finally said it was like a bucket of balls. Suddenly, I realized she was talking about a large plastic orange bucket of lacrosse balls that Dick had collected for Ricky to use while practicing his shots.

We were dumbfounded. How could a complete stranger in North Carolina, making a connection with us over the telephone, know what we had in the garage? It took about three minutes for us to even figure out what she was talking about, so how could she possibly know about the bucket of lacrosse balls?

My doubting husband started paying attention, and we all laughed, cried, and nodded our heads as she continued to share many warm, comforting messages of a very personal nature and meaning to us all. That reading was a turning point for Ann Marie, as Ricky repeatedly told her to go back to school and develop her artistic talents. He is very proud of her and wants her to live her life to the fullest. He encouraged her to do what she loves in life, and to not be afraid to express herself through her art.

One of Catherine's last statements to Dick, who kept expressing his amazement over the truth of the messages, was that we almost have to be shown miracles to believe that it's a true connection. She said, "If I were to tell you that in Ricky's closet is one red shoe, and you found a red shoe, then you'd believe." We laughed, hung up, and talked in amazement and wonder about the messages of love and peace from Catherine's reading. About two hours later, my husband walked into my office with his mouth open and eyes wide. He was holding one tennis shoe with red soles and stripes that he had just found in Ricky's closet!

Catherine advised us to keep watching for signs of communication, and for me to keep a detailed journal of what happened. She even suggested that I write a book! I laughed at that possibility, but as the months passed and my journal grew, I knew that I had to share our story with others.

We became aware of some endearing signs of Ricky's teasing presence about two months after he passed over. His friends loved to tell us many humorous stories about how he would bribe them to drive him places by offering them five dollars for a ride. When they picked him up, he would drop five dollars' worth of quarters in their laps. We, being the dumb parents, didn't know about Ricky raiding our change jar, although Dick did notice the level of change in his jar being a little low.

One warm day in March, Dick decided to clean up outside in the yard. He first tackled a pile of trash that we had stacked against our fence over the past three years. There were some large plastic bike jump ramps, two collapsed boating tubes, some trash, and an old bike stacked together.

Dick started throwing the trash in the back of his truck, and as he lifted the last water and leaf filled boating tube off the ground, he noticed a bright, shiny quarter lying on the ground where the tube had been. He thought that was rather unusual, but just put the quarter in his pocket and threw away the tubes. Next he went down onto the dock, which still was a mess from the fireworks on New Year's Eve. As he picked up some trash on the top deck, he found another bright, shiny quarter. Again he pocketed it and finished cleaning up. He came back into the house and went into Ricky's room to drop off some things he had found. I had just cleaned and vacuumed the room the day before, and nobody had been in there since. In the middle of the rug, waiting on him, was another bright, shiny quarter. With amazement, Dick pocketed the third quarter and came to show me his miraculous findings. We laughed, cried a little, and shook our heads at the typical humor of our son's little jokes on us.

We continued to find new, shiny quarters for a couple of months, and they always made us stop and laugh. Ricky just loved to tease, and we felt that in a small but humorous way he was trying to pay us back for the quarters he took.

The THINK key chains that we created also ended up serving as a communication tool for Ricky. The THINK lettering is made from a bright red vinyl material attached to the bronze lettering on the key chains. One day Ricky's last girlfriend sent us a message with a picture of her key chain. Her key chain had been transformed into a warm greeting from Ricky to her. The T, N, and K letters had dropped off, so in bright red letters across her key chain, right under the likeness of Ricky's face, were the letters: HI.

Not long after that, Dick looked at his key chain one day and realized that all the letters had dropped off except for the last one: K. We both chuckled at that one, since Ricky never said okay to us when we had a request or a demand. He always simply grunted, "K, Dad." That was definitely a message from beyond from our son.

HI keychain and K keychain

CHAPTER SEVEN
Ricky Roars

The poet Elizabeth Barrett Browning knew that at the end of this life, we return to pure Love. In her poem *I thought once how Theocritus had sung,* she says, "Guess now who holds thee? 'Death,' I said. But there the silver answer rang—not Death, but Love." She understood that when we pass from this Earth, we are joined with and become pure Love and Joy. Death is the beginning of our most exciting adventures!

James van Praagh, another famous psychic, has a video on his website of an interview he did with Mariel Hemingway. In that video, James wisely quips that "the biggest misconception about death is that you are dead!" We totally agree with him.

I am constantly amazed at how interconnected all of our thoughts, actions, and lives are. We usually aren't even aware how everything we do affects other people's lives, just like the ripple effect of throwing a rock into the water.

When Ricky was in fourth grade in Colorado, his class did a performance of the play *Hamlet*. I was puzzled when I saw that the teacher had assigned Ricky the part of the ghost of Hamlet's father. Ricky was such a loud, active, and outgoing child that it was unusual to see him playing the subdued role of a spirit who doesn't say anything in the first two appearances. I would like to tell that teacher how her simple assigning of roles in a fourth-grade play has affected our lives. Five years later, I was able to understand that it was meant to be for Ricky to play the part of a ghost who insists on coming back to deliver messages to his loved ones. Once again, there are no accidents in the Universe.

Over the past year and a half, we have had over thirty electronic communications from Ricky that have been witnessed by other people. We know that these communications are from Ricky since they happened either when we were talking about Ricky, honoring his memory, laughing about something that reminds us of him, or talking to other teens trying to help them understand that all our lives have a purpose. Ricky worked very hard to help us and those outside of our family realize that he is still with us, loving, laughing and assisting in our healing. We have been privileged to experience these communications of love from beyond.

During the first four months after Ricky passed, we were constantly being visited by his friends, boys and girls alike. Their presence was always was a great comfort to us and broke the silence of our empty home. Each time his military school friends walked through our door in their uniforms to raid our pantry, I could visualize Ricky following them with his bouncy walk, goofy grin, and booming voice demanding that all the Fruit Roll-Ups were his! Their laughter, energy, and animated stories about their daily lives and problems brought joy to our home, but there was usually so much noise and activity around them that we couldn't hear or focus on just one thing.

On April 17, 2010, four months after Ricky passed, we had an electrifying revelation. Mallory and Brooke, who had both known Ricky since kindergarten, came to visit us. It was Mallory's birthday, and they wanted to share with me the biggest, most sugar loaded cupcakes I had ever seen. These cupcakes were piled high with white, creamy frosting, and then covered with multicolored candy sprinkles. It was always a joke in our house about how much Ricky loved sweets covered with sprinkles. Every night before bed, he would get a bowl of ice cream and pour different types of sprinkles over the whole bowl. I never knew how he slept with so much sugar flooding his body.

As I opened the box of cupcakes the girls brought over and stared at the size of the cupcakes, I distinctly heard a lion roar sound in the living room. Like a bolt of lightning, I realized that I had been hearing that noise for a while. It usually sounded when his friends were at our house! With wide eyes and a huge grin, I looked at the girls and asked them if they heard that lion roar sound. They said they did. Suddenly serious, I looked straight at them, and declared, "I think that's Ricky!" Instantly, the lion roared again! If the lion hadn't roared immediately, I know both of the girls would have thought I had totally lost my mind.

I explained to them that I had just realized that I had been hearing that sound for several days whenever Ricky's friends came over. We looked at each other in shock and then burst into laughter. Both of the girls knew about our pelican visitations, and Mallory jokingly said, "Well, a lion's certainly a better symbol for Ricky than a pelican!" She was absolutely right—our son's spirit definitely resembles a proud lion, and it is so fitting that he chose that animal's sound to communicate with us.

I immediately wrote in my journal what happened. I decided from then on to document the date we heard the lion roar, what was happening or being said right before the lion roared, and who was with us to witness these amazing communications. We were so thrilled that our strong-willed, clever son figured out this unique way to soothe our aching hearts. He was letting us know immediately that he was right there with us, listening, watching, laughing with us, and loving us all.

The pelicans, quarters, dreams, visions, and messages from the psychic were comforting, but the lion roars were a real, indisputable source of contact with our son—an instant feedback that let us know he was still with us, just in another form that we couldn't see, and right there in the room with us roaring his approval.

Before I continue with our astounding incidents, I need to describe the source of the lion roar sound. We have two grandchildren who visit frequently, and I have two wooden puzzles for them that I keep on the open bottom shelf of our coffee table in the living room. One of these wooden puzzles is a handcrafted sound puzzle. It has eight removable pieces with various animals painted on them and small round red knobs to lift them up. A light sensor is in the base of the wooden puzzle, centered in each animal shape's place in the base. As you lift out the animal shape, then return it to its proper place, the wooden piece blocks the light for the sensor and activates the puzzle to make that animal's sound. The puzzle makes the sounds for a monkey, penguin, parrot, zebra, elephant, snake, alligator, and a lion. As is usual with children's toys, some of the animal shapes were missing—the lion and the penguin.

I hadn't tried to analyze how the puzzle worked, but after hearing the lion roar, I decided to conduct some experiments. As bizarre as it sounds that our son's spirit could activate the lion roaring sound, I could not find any way to activate the sound without actually covering the sensor with my hand for at least three seconds. I tried jumping around in front of it to see if it was movement activated, waving my hand back and forth over the sensor, sliding the base around under the table to see if it was motion activated, and moving the whole puzzle out onto the top of the table. Nothing makes the lion roar other than covering the sensor for about three seconds. It seems to be just a simple puzzle, but it has made a life-changing difference in our lives as well as the lives of several of Ricky's friends.

sound puzzle

One day Brooke, who had been with us that first day when we realized the source of the lion roar, visited us. She had been in a bad car accident, and she felt that Ricky had been her guardian angel who kept her from getting seriously hurt. As she showed us her injury and repeatedly told us that she felt certain that Ricky had protected her, the lion roared. Her smile lit up the room as she acknowledged his love. By this time, Ricky's friends had heard about all our signs and communications, and they were always amazed and delighted. Ricky was a very popular, vibrant friend, and they were having a hard time getting through their days without his joyful presence.

A few weeks later, Thomas, one of Ricky's military school friends decided to visit us by himself to talk about his progress with learning how to play lacrosse. Over twenty of Ricky's school friends, from seniors down to freshmen, had picked up lacrosse after his death to honor his passion and dedication to the growth of the sport in our town. We were talking to this friend and encouraging him to participate in a lacrosse clinic that Dick had organized with the Army lacrosse team coach. We felt it was an incredible opportunity for Ricky's friend to learn a lot from a very accomplished coach in a short time period, but he was reluctant to sign up since he was so new to the sport. As soon as we said, "Just do it!" all three of us very clearly heard the lion roar. Thomas' face lit up with amazement, and he said, "Was that Ricky?" As we all laughed together, we told him we were sure that was Ricky roaring his approval for his friend to sign up for the camp. He laughed loudly and said, "Ricky always told me, 'Don't be such a girl!'" What a sense of humor!

In May, Mallory came to visit us again. Mallory had known Ricky since he was four and felt like a big sister to him. We had been out of town for a few days, and Dick was in his office checking his e-mail messages. Dick came into the kitchen where we were sitting and started telling us about the recent senior graduation ceremony at Ricky's military high school. With great pride, he told us that the school played "Taps" at the ceremony in Ricky's honor— and the lion instantly roared. We looked at each other with wonder, for we knew this was Ricky acknowledging how proud he was of his school brothers, and how touched he was by the seniors at his school honoring a freshman.

Each time Dick and I heard our son roar his approval or laughter, all we could do was look at each other and shake our heads in amazement. At the same time we celebrated such an overwhelmingly happy event, we also were so flooded with the emotional pain of how much we missed him that it was difficult. We eventually realized that every time we experienced his communications, our pain was pushed farther and farther away from our minds as he showed us how close we still were. We have no idea how Ricky is able to manipulate the sound puzzle to contact us, but it makes us proud that he loves us so much that he's figured out a way to stay in touch.

Later in May, two more of our daughter's friends were visiting us. They wanted some of our THINK key chains to carry with them. As I gave them each a key chain, we started looking at Ricky's face on the key chains. Due to the bronzing process, it's not an exact likeness, but the smile is just as big and goofy. Ricky was a very good-looking boy, and he always used to laughingly say, "I'm a sexy beast!" One of the girls commented that the face on the key chain didn't look as good as Ricky's real face did, and Ricky immediately roared!

Although Ricky's friends' visits were comforting and filled with care, I missed having a young life around to nourish, love, and snuggle with. Even though Ricky was fifteen and well past snuggling age, I missed being around my youngest—my baby. In May, our daughter came home from college, and she and I picked out a Boxer puppy to bring home. What a wonderful time we had carrying around that little warm bundle of fur with sweet kisses and puppy breath to make us smile. Over the next few weeks, we realized what we had been missing around the house—that endless, restless energy that Ricky always exuded. Somehow we had picked a puppy that brought that same type of energy into the house. She was a bundle of love and playful energy, and laughter was constant in our house again. Ricky's friends loved coming by to play with her, and one day three of them were at our house wrestling with her. As we all joked about how much the puppy reminded us of being around Ricky, Ricky roared!

We had Ricky's body cremated and had planned for months to take part of him home to his beloved Colorado. We all knew that his spirit was flying free and happy, but we felt strongly that he would want to be part of his favorite snowboard jump in the terrain park. In July we flew out to Colorado with George and his wife, Ann Marie and her boyfriend, and some of Ricky's ashes. We had a wonderful week of hiking, white water rafting, visiting with old, good friends, and reminiscing over what a wonderful life we had with our Ricky.

Our best friends in Colorado had two children our children's ages, and while living there, all eight of us became best friends. Their children spent as much time at our house as they did at their own. They all played sports together, and Dick and their father coached several of their team sports. It is a wonderful, lifelong friendship for us all, and it was very sad for Ricky's best friend to not have him around anymore. We tried not to talk about the hole in our "combined family."

We picked a sparkling clear day to hike up to the terrain park with our extended family of friends, then slipped and skidded our way to the edge of what remained of the ice packed snowboard jump. We laughed, cried, and goofed around for the camera as we all said our goodbyes to him while tossing some of his ashes into the slight breeze. It was a true bittersweet moment.

Later that day, Ann Marie, some of her Colorado girlfriends, her boyfriend, and Ricky's best friend were in the living room just hanging out. By that time, I didn't go anywhere without our beloved sound puzzle, for we didn't want to miss any chance of more communications with Ricky.

Dick and I had gone out, and I had left the puzzle board sitting on the top of the kitchen counter, along with some other things the kids had strewn around. Ricky's best friend, Max, didn't know about our lion roaring experiences, and as he was walking past the kitchen counter, he saw the puzzle sitting there. He stepped toward it with his hands out to pick it up and said, "What's this?" With split second timing, right before his hands closed around the puzzle to pick it up, Ricky roared! Max jumped back, alarmed, and said, "Whoooaaa!" After Ann Marie explained to everyone the source of the lion roar, the kids laughingly commented on this typical example of Ricky's fondness for playing jokes on his friends.

They all spent several hours that day hanging around in the kitchen, messing around with each other's laptops, and just catching up with each other. Ann Marie's boyfriend left the room for a while to change clothes, and the girls immediately pounced on his laptop. They giggled and joked as they created a new screensaver for him, with unicorns, pink bunnies, flowers, and a rainbow in a green meadow. As soon as our daughter's boyfriend came back into the room and laughed over what they had done to his screensaver, Ricky roared again! These examples of his teasing personality let all his good friends know that he was right there with them, joining in on the humor and good times together.

In October Ann Marie came home from college to celebrate her birthday and brought some friends home with her. They enjoyed a clear, starlit night outside by the fire pit, cooking S'mores and talking late into the night with some of her local friends. Several of Ricky's friends have adopted her as their "sister," so they also came over to join in the good times and cookout. The next morning we were all in the kitchen talking about what they had done the night before, how many friends were there, and how much fun they had being together again. Instantly, Ricky roared! Ricky always loved being outdoors, by a fire, and hanging out with his sister's older girlfriends. He was letting us know how much he loves Ann Marie and her expanded circle of friends.

These after death communications have happened at different times of the day, with different people around, in different cities, whether the puzzle was near a source of light or in the dark, and whether Dick and I were present or not. The timing of the roars has always been an instant feedback of our son's awareness of what was going on around us. They have served to help us understand that he is still with us, sharing his love and concern for us.

He's just in another form of energy.

CHAPTER EIGHT

A Future with Hope

Jeremiah 29:11 declares, "For surely I know the plans I have for you, says the Lord, plans for your welfare and not for harm, to give you a future with hope." Dick and I used the power of faith and our positive thoughts to help get us through our toughest trials, and we found our inner strength.

We have shared our experiences with wonder and awe to demonstrate the divine love that surrounds us. It's true for all of us: we only need to ask for help and believe.

Our continued signs and communications from our son are not only a testimony of his love and compassion for us, but they have also had tremendous healing power, both for us and the others who know about them. We have not searched them out; they are God's and Ricky's gifts to us.

Our agony, our tears, our doubts have all been eased and soothed by the love that we now know surrounds us daily. Psalm 40: 1-3 affirms, "I waited patiently for the Lord, and he inclined unto me, and heard my cry. He brought me up also out of a horrible pit, out of the miry clay, and set my feet upon a rock, and established my goings. And he hath put a new song in my mouth." Our faith is our song and our gratitude is our rock.

Our pain and suffering did lead to more good than negative. We have grown—in knowledge, in strength and in faith. Hope has been reborn in our hearts. There is no doubt that we are better, kinder, and more compassionate souls than before.

When you have sunk to the deepest pits of despair, felt your heart torn into pieces, and struggled to claw your way back to living and loving again, you have won the hardest battle of all. The great football coach Vince Lombardi said, "The *real* glory is being knocked to your knees, then coming back."

We now feel that we can see the purpose for the rest of our lives and are at peace with Ricky's short life. We understand that he was given the gifts of so much unusual joy, talent, charm, and accomplishment in this lifetime because God knew that his time here would be condensed. One of Ricky's life's purposes was to show us how to fully enjoy our time here, and how to live a life filled with joy, love and gusto. He woke up every morning looking forward to what new adventure that day would bring, never met a person he didn't immediately befriend, never held a grudge, and filled every day of his life with fun, friends and laughter. I can't think of a life better lived.

If Dick and I were to be offered today the choice of only having fifteen years with our son or never having known him at all, we would choose without hesitation to relive every moment of our wonderful short years with him. As hard as it has been to accept what happened, our personal growth, our new understanding of how the Universe works, and what we can share with others from our experiences have been to our benefit.

We now realize the importance of making the most of every moment while we're still here to do whatever we can to help others. All our lives are so interwoven with ways that we can either help or hurt each other that we must try to always consider how our words and actions will affect others. Whatever we put out in this life is what we will attract, so our purity of thought, word and action is vital to our own quality of life.

On the time clock of eternity, our presence here is very short, so we have to share love whenever we can. In 1 Peter, 3:8, we are advised, "Finally, all of you, have unity of spirit, sympathy, love for one another, a tender heart, and a humble mind."

In Sogyal Rinpoche's preface to *The Tibetan Book of Living and Dying*, he states that every religion teaches some type of life after death. We shouldn't be afraid of the inevitable. We shouldn't have to wait for the death of a loved one to force us into looking at our lives. We should use our lives to prepare for our death, not avoid it. We should make every moment count toward making ourselves—our spiritual selves, our souls—stronger, better, and kinder. Rinpoche says, "That goodness is what survives. The whole of our life is a teaching of how to uncover that strong goodness, and is a training towards realizing it."

Have no fear of death—it isn't an ending. It's the beginning of our real lives with eternal, true love and peace.

Dick and I have refocused our lives. We have chosen to make a positive difference in the lives of others. We have founded a nonprofit organization, the Ricky McAllaster Foundation, to promote teen driving safety programs in our area, plus help promote youth amateur sports. Inexperienced teenage driving is the number one cause of teen deaths in our country. Our website, *http://www.RIP-ten.com*, is dedicated to our efforts to honor our son by keeping other teens safe.

The THINK key chains that were inspired by our experience with the policeman the night Ricky passed gave us the idea to make exit signs for all the high schools in our area. The exit signs have a large picture of the key chain saying THINK in red reflective letters diagonally across Ricky's face, then on the bottom in red reflective letters is printed DRIVE HOME SAFELY. Every parent who has seen these exit signs feels they should be posted at the exit of all schools across the nation.

THINK exit signs

We have organized an annual lacrosse tournament in Savannah, Georgia to raise funds for our Ricky McAllaster Foundation, with college, high school, middle school, and under eleven teams participating. Our community's support is overwhelming and inspiring. We have been shown over and over again how good people are through the love, compassion, and comfort so many have given us.

Dick has been coaching both high school and middle school lacrosse to help introduce other boys to this incredible sport that our son was so passionate about. Dick is on the Board of Ricky's high school, is the head coach for the varsity lacrosse team, and is thrilled to participate with Ricky's friends life experiences. We may have lost the physical presence of our son, but we have gained the gift of watching so many other boys find a passion in their lives.

I help with the fund-raising and organization of the tournament, minister to friends when they lose a loved one, spend as much time as I can with family and friends, have found inspiration, love and spiritual growth in our local Unity church, and have now learned how to write and publish a book! I have shifted my passion for horses from showing for personal satisfaction to working as a volunteer with local Hippotherapy riding programs. The bravery of these special children and the huge smiles of joy on their faces as they ride a horse never fails to lift my spirits in thanks to God for this chance to serve others.

As we continue to grow and witness the good that has come from our son's passing, our marriage has become stronger than ever. The divorce rate for couples who have lost a child is almost ninety percent, but we couldn't imagine not having each other to lean on. There is no other person on earth who could imagine or fully understand what we have lost or what we have gained through our experiences. We encourage each other in whatever project we undertake to help others, and work together toward that mission. Our lives are filled with purpose and meaning.

The albatross of grief has been lifted from our souls.

Ann Marie has changed her college major to Art and has actually started a clothing line named RIP 10. Ricky always picked number ten as his number in sports, which was appropriate since he was usually the high point scorer.

The number ten is very appropriate for us, as it symbolizes both an end and a new beginning (it is the end of single digits and the beginning of double digits). Last May, Dick was trying to pick out gifts for his middle school players for their end of season party. He decided it would be fun to create a wild, crazy line of lacrosse clothes that our son would love. Ricky liked anything different and attention-getting! As soon as Dick mentioned that idea, I realized that Ann Marie's designs, which she had been creating for years, would be perfect. So RIP 10 lacrosse clothes has been created, is for sale on eBay, our website (http://*www.RIP-10.com*) and on Lax.com. Ann Marie has a new career in only her sophomore year of college.

Dick and I daily try to honor how our lives are so interconnected, and how our choices affect other's lives so much. We are constantly reminded that there are no accidents; everything happens for a purpose.

Because Don helped us in our time of sorrow, he is now unretired and continuing his passion for preaching God's word. Our policeman friend who gave Dick the bronze coin now has two of our THINK key chains and glow in the dark wristbands for his teenage children's driving safety. My father advised a local Ford car dealer on how to start his business and that dealer is now helping us get connected with Ford's Driving Skills for Life program so we can try to bring it into our area's high schools. Countless parents have contacted us to thank us for the key chains and wristbands, for their children have stopped to think after drinking at a party and called for a ride home. Several of these parents were the ones who helped organize a steady stream of food to be delivered to our house in those first cold, pain-filled months. The repeated theme of how showing love and compassion for others ends up coming back to help us is amazing. Whatever you give out comes back to you tenfold.

Ricky, always # 10

We now look forward to what daily inspiring situations will be presented to us. Our days are filled with hope and activity, plans for continuing our incredible son's legacy, and chances to meet people to share love with. Our search for peace from excruciating pain and loss has thankfully ended with faith and trust in God's perfect plan for us.

Our continued communications from Ricky aren't as frequent as they were, but we're ok with that. We have been shown that he is always involved in our lives. Our wonderful Ricky is still with us, and will be first in line waiting for us when we pass over.

Trust in this—love never ends.

"Silently, one by one, in the infinite meadows of Heaven, blossom the lovely stars, the forget-me-nots of angels."—Henry Wadsworth Longfellow

REFERENCES

The Holy Bible, the 1928 Book of Common Prayer, Preservation Press, Swedesboro, New Jersey: Psalm 91:4, Isiah 6:8, Jeremiah 29:11, Psalm 40: 1-3, 1st Peters 3:8.

Browning, Elizabeth Barrett. *I thought once how Theocritus had sung, Sonnets from the Portuguese, 1840, lines 13-14.*

Char, *Questions from Earth, Answers from Heaven,* p. 47.

Dickerson, Matt, *http://www.thednaoflife.com, Faith, Your Thought,Love*, April 18, 2009.

Longfellow, Henry Wadsworth. *Evangeline, A Tale of Arcadie,* Part 1, Canto III, 1893.

Praagh, James. *http://www.vanpraagh.com, Tune into the Spiritual World* video, January, 2011.

Rinpoche, Sogyal, *The Tibetan Book of Living and Dying.* Harper 1, New York, New York, p. 86.

Suarez, Lee. *God doesn't give you the people you want,* quote from http://www.goodreads.com/quotes.

Wikipedia.org. *Law of conservation of energy, First Law of Thermodynamics.*